The Shoemakes:
God's Helpers

ELSIE RIVES

Illustrated by Dick Wahl

BROADMAN PRESS
Nashville, Tennessee

Thanks

To Dorothy Dell and Howard for being God's missionaries and for sharing the story of their lives with me.

To Mrs. "M." (Marie Mathis) who taught me to love missionaries and missions work.

To Ana Shaw, my seven-year-old great-niece, who helped me write the book.

© Copyright 1986 • Broadman Press

All rights reserved

4243-28

ISBN: 0-8054-4328-2

Dewey Decimal Classification: J266.092

Subject Headings: SHOEMAKE, HOWARD L. / / SHOEMAKE, DOROTHY DELL / /

MISSIONS—LATIN AMERICA

Library of Congress Catalog Card Number: 86-2603

Printed in the United States of America

Library of Congress Cataloging-in-Publication Data

Rives, Elsie.
   The Shoemakes: God's helpers.

   (Meet the missionary series)
   Summary: Relates how Howard and Dorothy Shoemake
accepted the call to become missionaries in Latin
America and describes their work there and the
people whom they help.
   1. Shoemake, Howard—Juvenile literature.
   2. Shoemake, Dorothy—Juvenile literature.
   3. Missionaries—Latin America—Biography—Juvenile
literature.   4. Missionaries—United States—Biography—
Juvenile literature.   5. Missions—Latin America—Juven-
ile literature.   [1. Shoemake, Howard.   2. Shoemake,
Dorothy.   3. Missionaries.   4. Missions—Latin
America] I. Wahl, Richard, 1939–   ill.   II. Title.
III. Series.
BV2832.R58   1986   266'.0092'2 [B] [920]   86-2603
ISBN 0-8054-4328-2

Contents

A Boy Named Howard 5
A Girl Called Dorothy Dell 7
School Days 14
A Country Called Colombia 16
Learning a New Language 21
A Country Called Ecuador 22
Moving to a New Country 25
Saving the Babies 28
The Work Goes On 30
Remember 32
About the Author 32

A Boy Named Howard

"Howard," called his mother. "Howard, Howard." No answer came.

"Howard Lee Shoemake, come here now."

At the sound of his full name, Howard came running and laughing. He was a happy boy. He liked to tease his mother. He liked to have fun.

Howard was tall and large for his age. The first morning he went to kindergarten he cried. "I don't want to be in this room with babies," he yelled.

The principal let Howard go to the first grade. There he was with boys and girls his own size. But not going to kindergarten made first grade harder for Howard.

Howard and his younger brother, Earl, walked to Sunday School. Howard did not always behave in Sunday School. Sometimes he did not listen to the teacher. He disturbed the class. But Howard did learn about God. He learned God loved him.

One Sunday when Howard was nine, he became a Christian. That was a special day for him. He wanted to tell everyone, "I am a Christian. I believe in Jesus," he told his friends. But his friends were not interested.

When Howard was sixteen, he went to church camp. His best friend, Udell Smith, went to camp too. He and Howard got into mischief several times. Once when everyone had gone to bed, Howard and Udell got up. They tried to leave the camp grounds. The night watchman caught them at the gate. He took them to the camp director.

"You have disobeyed the rules," said the camp director. "I will have to send you home."

The night watchman wanted the boys to have one more chance. He asked the director to let them stay.

Later that week, Howard made an important decision. "I feel God is asking me to be a preacher," he told Dr. Cauthen, the camp pastor.

Howard went home from camp. He told his parents about his decision.

"Howard, we are happy you want to be a preacher," his mother said. "Before you were born, your father and I prayed. We asked God to give us a son. We promised to help our son love and serve God. God has answered our prayers."

A Girl Called Dorothy Dell

"Lord, give us a baby," Mr. and Mrs. Moore prayed. "We will guide this child to love and serve you." In time, God answered their prayers.

On a cool October day, a baby girl was born. They named her Dorothy Dell.

Dorothy Dell was a shy girl. She liked the farm on which she lived. She liked to ride on the back of the wagon with her father. Horses pulled the wagon through the fields.

"Don't sit too close to the edge of the wagon," her father warned. "You may fall and hurt yourself."

Dorothy Dell heard her father. "I will not fall," she thought. But one day the horses were pulling the wagon very fast. The wheels ran over a rock.

Suddenly, Dorothy Dell fell out of the wagon. She landed on top of a prickly-pear bush.

Oh, how the stickers hurt! Carefully, her father picked the stickers from her arms and legs.

Dorothy Dell remembered what her father had said. She learned a lot that day. "Parents do know the best for us," Dorothy Dell thought.

On Sundays, Dorothy Dell went to church with her parents. Grandma Kirtley was Dorothy Dell's Sunday School teacher. Each Sunday she gave Dorothy Dell a picture card. On it was a Bible story picture and a Bible verse. These cards were very special to Dorothy Dell.

Dorothy Dell walked several miles to school. To save time, she often cut through a pasture where a bull was kept.

Some mornings the bull would chase Dorothy
Dell. She would run to the fence and climb over
quickly. Sometimes her dress would catch on the
fence and tear. Often she would be crying when
she got to school.

Dorothy Dell was smart and liked to learn. But
she didn't like going to school very much. After a
time, Dorothy Dell grew to love her teachers. She
found that school could be fun.

At home, Dorothy Dell had a special playhouse behind the garage. She used boxes for tables and chairs. She picked wild flowers to put in vases on the tables. She served mud pies on cracked dishes. Dorothy Dell liked to play house in the yard. One afternoon her mother came to visit her.

"May I come in?" Mrs. Moore asked.

"Yes, please do," said Dorothy Dell.

Mrs. Moore sat on one box. Dorothy Dell sat on a box facing her.

"I have come to talk to you about how to become a Christian," her mother said. Mrs. Moore opened her Bible and read. She told Dorothy Dell about God's love and His plan. She talked about Jesus.

Dorothy Dell understood. That night at the revival service she told the church she was a Christian. Soon she was baptized in a river near the church.

In high school, Dorothy Dell felt God was asking her to do more for Him. She told her friends, "I know God wants me to do something special for Him. I do not know now what it will be."

School Days

Dorothy Dell Moore and Howard Lee Shoemake went to college. They went to Howard Payne College in Brownwood, Texas, in January, 1939.

When they first met, they didn't like each other very much. But those feelings changed. They worked well together in missions work in the town. They spent lots of time talking. Soon they realized they loved each other.

"Dorothy Dell, I want to marry you," said Howard. "I want us to spend our lives together." They were married in a beautiful church service, December 29, 1940.

Dorothy Dell and Howard finished college together. Then they entered the seminary in Fort Worth, Texas. But soon Howard became restless. He wanted to preach. He left the seminary to become the pastor at the First Baptist Church of Navasota, Texas.

One Sunday Dr. Baker James Cauthen was preaching in their church. "We need preachers to be missionaries to go to other countries. Some people have never heard about Jesus," he said.

After the service, Dorothy Dell and Howard talked with Dr. Cauthen.

"I feel you are thinking about going to another country as a missionary," said Dr. Cauthen.

A happy look came to Howard's face. "Yes," he answered. "I want to go to places where people do not know about Jesus."

The decision was made. Dorothy Dell and Howard would return to the seminary to finish their studies. Then they would go to a foreign land as missionaries.

A Country Called Colombia

"Will you go to the country of Colombia?" asked the Foreign Mission Board. "We need you there so some of the missionaries can come home for a furlough."

Howard, Dorothy Dell, and their two sons, David and Glenn, were soon in their new home in Barranquilla, Colombia [BAH-ran-key-ah, Coh-lom-bee-ah].

Everything was different. The people spoke Spanish. But the Shoemakes did not.

The people of the churches loved the new missionaries and their boys. Although they could not talk to each other, they smiled a lot.

In church the Shoemake family heard music to songs they knew. They heard "Jesus Loves Me," but the words were very different.

Christo me ama

[crees-toh may ah-mah]

Christo me ama

Christo me ama

La Biblia di-ce asi.

[la bee-blee-ah dee-say ah-see]

The Shoemakes began to learn Spanish from a teacher. They learned Spanish words from the church people and others with whom they worked.

Many people in Colombia were learning about Jesus. The churches were growing. The missionaries knew they needed buildings in which to work.

"Howard," they said, "we need schools, pastors' homes, and a hospital. Will you build them?"

Howard was a preacher, not a builder of buildings. But he started to work. He knew God needed him to do this special job.

Each day Howard worked on the new buildings. At night he preached to the people in the churches.

Dorothy Dell was busy as a missionary too. She worked in her home with her family. On Sundays she taught the younger boys and girls in Sunday School. Many of them heard about Jesus for the first time. Older girls came to missions meetings. They heard about God and what He wanted them to do.

After church services, Dorothy Dell opened the book store in the church. She helped the people to get Christian books to read in the Spanish language.

"I enjoy working in the book store," Dorothy Dell would say. "I want the people to have Christian books to read."

Four years passed. Dorothy Dell and Howard prayed about their work. They knew God had other things for them to do. They wrote to the Foreign Mission Board about going to another place where people did not know Jesus. They wanted to learn Spanish better. At last, a message came from the Foreign Mission Board.

"We need you in a country called Ecuador. You may have extra time to go to school to study the Spanish language."

Learning a New Language

"Buenas dias." (Good morning [bway-nas dee-ahs])

"Buenas tardes." (Good afternoon [bway-nas tar-days])

"Buenas noches." (Good night [bway-nas no-chess])

"Venga a mi casa." (Come to my house [van-gah ah mee KAH-sah])

Howard and Dorothy Dell were learning how to speak Spanish. They were in language school in Costa Rica.

Many missionary families were there learning Spanish. They wanted to be able to tell people who spoke Spanish about Jesus.

Everyone spoke Spanish at the school. The teachers taught in Spanish. All day long the missionaries spoke the Spanish language.

Howard and Dorothy Dell learned much about the Spanish words. They learned to speak, read, and preach in the Spanish language.

A Country Called Ecuador

Language school was over. The Shoemake family traveled to Ecuador. They were excited when they arrived in their new place of work.

"This is a beautiful place. We can look out and see the ocean," exclaimed the boys.

"Yes, it is beautiful," said their father. "And there are many people here who need to hear about Jesus."

Howard made friends with some of the men in the city. As he worked with them, some became Christians. These men told their wives and families about Jesus. They, too, became Christians.

Before long Dorothy Dell invited some women to her home. They met to study the Bible. They learned from the Bible. They taught their children. More people became Christians.

Soon Howard found a building he could rent. The church began to meet there to study and worship God. Many men came to the church building at five in the morning. Howard taught them the Bible. He helped them learn about the work of the church. Some men became

Christians. They told others about Jesus. The church grew.

"God is so good," Dorothy Dell and Howard said. "Great things are beginning to happen in Ecuador."

At times all did not go well for the Shoemake family. Three-year-old Jimmy fell from a very high balcony in the building where they lived. His arms were broken. His head was hurt. The doctors in the hospital said that Jimmy might not live.

"Dear God," prayed the people in the church, "please help Jimmy get well."

The family talked to God. The doctors worked. Jimmy began to get well.

"Thank you, God, for helping Jimmy," they prayed. Many people believed in God because of what He had done for Jimmy.

Good things also happened to the Shoemakes. They now had four boys. Their names were David, Glenn, Jimmy, and Rickey. In October, a baby girl was born. They named her Carol. Everyone loved her.

Mr. and Mrs. Shoemake were always very busy
with missionary work. But they found days for
family fun. The family would go to the beautiful,
sandy beaches on the Pacific Ocean. They would
swim and lie in the sun. At lunch-time, they
would have a picnic on the beach.

Howard enjoyed taking pictures with his
camera. A student in the university who was
studying to be a doctor learned about Howard's
pictures. "Will you take pictures for me? I want to
use them in my paper called a thesis," asked the
student.

Howard really did not have time to take the pictures, but this young doctor was not a Christian. Howard wanted to tell him about Jesus.

So, Howard began to make the pictures. As they worked together, Howard told the doctor about Jesus. The doctor believed and became a Christian.

This doctor told others about Jesus. Many of the young student doctors became Christians.

Moving to a New Country

One night Howard could not sleep. He slipped quietly out of bed. He took his Bible from the table. He began to read from Isaiah. God was giving him a message.

"I will let you tell presidents and leaders about Me. I will guide you. I will take care of you."

Howard read and talked to God all night. God helped him know what to do.

In the early morning, Howard woke Dorothy Dell. "I know God wants us to go to a new country to work," he said to her. "I will tell the Foreign Mission Board how I feel."

"Yes," came the answer from the Foreign Mission Board. "We need you to start a new mission work on the island called the Dominican Republic."

The Shoemakes and their children were ready to go to the new country. This was a special challenge. So many people needed to know about Jesus.

Howard brought a ham radio set with him. With it, he could talk to people all over the world.

Through the radio, Howard made many friends. He attended a radio club. The members were not Christians. They liked Howard, the Baptist preacher. Two friends helped Howard start religious radio and television programs.

"We need a church building where we can meet to worship and learn about God," Howard decided. He looked around. Soon he found a large building. He rented it for the church. In Spanish it was called Templo Bautista Central.

Dorothy Dell had a book deposit, like a book store, in her living room at home. She sold Christian books and Bibles to the people and to other book stores.

Dorothy Dell liked to visit and give out Spanish literature. These pieces of material told people about the Bible and how to become a Christian.

The people of the Dominican Republic loved Howard and Dorothy Dell. The two missionaries showed everyone they met what loving Jesus could do.

Saving the Babies

Howard noticed that many babies in the Dominican Republic were sick and dying. This made him very sad. He wanted to find out what he could do to help. He talked on his ham radio to a medical group in the United States.

"Will you send medicine to help the babies get well?" Howard asked.

"Yes," they replied. "You must work with the doctors to get the medicine to the babies. You must direct the work."

Howard worked with the minister of health and the president of the Dominican Republic. He got permission to set up the first places for the doctors to work.

Medical clinics were set up all over the country. Hundreds came to the clinics each day. The mothers held their babies while the doctors gave them the medicine they needed to get well.

As Howard helped the babies, he showed the doctors how Jesus worked in his life. Nine doctors became Christians. They were baptized and came to church.

People all over the country loved the Shoemake family. The Shoemakes had done much to help the people.

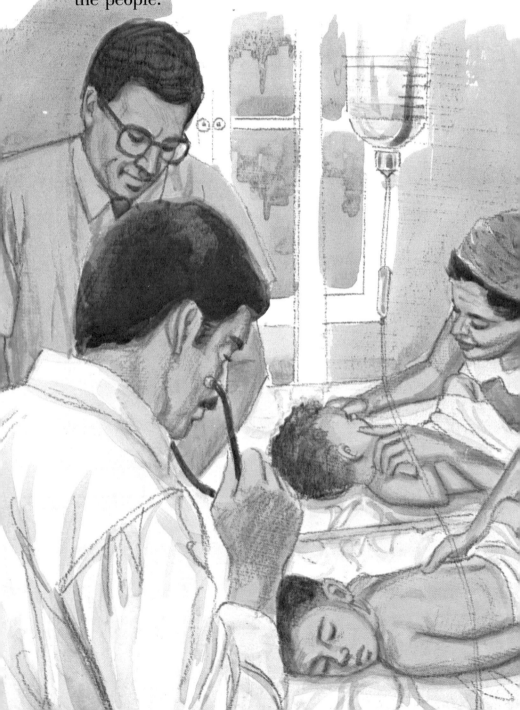

The Work Goes On

Howard and Dorothy Dell Shoemake worked as missionaries in the Dominican Republic for eighteen years. They helped people know about Jesus. In many ways they helped people who needed them.

Howard received the highest award given by the Dominican Republic. The award was called, "The badge of the order of *Duarte, Sánchez and Mella*." It was given in recognition of Howard's work. He was made a "son of the Republic."

The people knew that Howard had done all of these good things because he loved Jesus. Dorothy Dell and their five children had worked with him as missionaries.

In November 1980, it was time for Howard and Dorothy Dell to retire. They left the Dominican Republic to live in Texas.

The Shoemakes joined the Shiloh Terrace Baptist Church in Dallas, Texas. The church has a home for missionaries. The church calls the home, "The Howard and Dorothy Dell Shoemake Cottage."

At the time, Howard Shoemake was very ill. On May 6, 1983, Howard died. He was God's special helper all of his life.

Dorothy Dell Shoemake lives in Garland, Texas, near her five children. They are grown now and married. She has ten grandchildren. Their names are Kevin J., Deidrea, Daniel, Angela, Caleb, Jennifer, Rebecca, Rachel, Kevin T., and Steven.

"God is good," says Mrs. Shoemake. "There is joy in getting up each morning. God wants us day by day to be his helpers."

Remember

God helped Dorothy Dell and Howard get ready to work for Him. They went to church to learn about God. They became Christians. They learned how to tell others about God.

God helped Dorothy Dell and Howard find each other. He guided them to get married and live their lives together.

God led the Shoemakes to be missionaries in Colombia, Ecuador, and the Dominican Republic.

God will help you know what to do if you trust Him and ask Him to guide you. Ask God to help you become what He wants you to be.

About the Author

Elsie Rives lives in Nashville, Tennessee. If you came to see her, she probably would not be at home. She travels around the United States teaching workers with children about Sunday School. She enjoys teaching boys and girls in her church. They are special friends.